Economics in an Afternoon

By Scott R. Hasserd

Contents

Scott R. Hasserd

Preface

During my studies as an
undergrad in Economics at North
Carolina State University, I
learned that Economics was quite
a unique subject in many ways.
The most unique and paradoxical
thing about it being, that
somehow most people I have
encountered believe two things
about economics: it is complex or
boring, and they know all they

Economics in an Afternoon

need to know about it. Think

about it: the economy is often one

of the largest topics of debates

between candidates and voters,

yet take any one of these

politicians or voters and ask them

to give a cohesive and concise

description or theory of how the

economy works, from the most

basic level of an single person to

the global level, and see how deep

that description goes, beyond

campaign talking points and

clichés. Where does money come

from? Why do we need it? Where

Scott R. Hasserd

do jobs come from? Why do we trade with other countries? One thing is true about Economics: it is complex, though it need not be boring, it can be one of the most fascinating topics due to its connection to fields such as psychology, sociology, the natural world, politics, and many other areas of study.

My goal in this book is to provide my understanding of economics, based on what I gleaned during my education from reading various economists such

Economics in an Afternoon

as Milton Friedman, F.A. Hayek,

Bastiat, Hazlitt, and Mises, in

order to provide a basic

understanding of economics to

anyone who wants to get started

on the subject as well as inspire

them to learn more about it.

There was more that

could have gone into this book,

though it is only meant to give a

brief, foundation to understand

economics and hopefully inspire

many to learn more about how

economies work.

Scott R. Hasserd

What is Economics?

Simply put, economics is the study of how people, with varying wants and needs, make choices to accomplish those wants and attain those needs: I have an apple and want a banana, you have a banana and want an apple; let's make a deal. This deal, or compromise rather, is not completely the best scenario for either one of us in particular; the best scenario for me would be if you gave me the banana and I kept the apple and the opposite would be the best scenario for you, though by making this trade freely we have satisfied both of our wants with a compromise we can both agree on.

This trading between individuals has a unique element in it: the transfer of goods is mutually agreed upon, otherwise it would not occur. No one was robbed or harmed by this trade, though if there was the use of any force, deceit, or other dishonest practices used by either party then that's a different, darker story that will be addressed later.

Now our little trade earlier works well if you and I are the only two people trading only two goods, but what if there are more people and more goods involved?

Let us say that I have an apple and want a banana, you have a banana but want an orange. Now I must find someone who has an orange, and wants an

Economics in an Afternoon

apple, in order to trade with you. That string of trades is still doable, but what if we scale this example up even more, and you and I started wanting more than just fruit, what if we want computers, cars, steaks, and clothes. Well that is going to require a lot of intermediate trading just to make the final trade we want. Now imagine that instead of one apple for one orange to get one banana, that it takes two apples to get 1 orange that we could use to get half a banana, so now I must trade 4 apples for 2 oranges to get one banana. So now we both must keep track of who wants a particular good and who has a particular good, as well as how valuable each of these goods are in relation to each other, thus creating a vast matrix of goods and their relative values to one another. The solution developed for this complexity was the use of currency (i.e. money).

What is Money?

Money or currency is a medium of exchange. It is something that allows two people, with different wants and needs, to make a trade that both can agree on. If we introduce money to our previous example, suddenly it becomes much simpler. I must simply find someone willing to pay for an apple and I can then use the money to buy a banana from you, and you can go and buy an orange. Additionally, the only two values both of us must keep track of is how valuable the goods we want and have are in relation to money. And instead of having a complex matrix of prices to keep track of, every item is neatly tied to a monetary amount, or price.

Well now you might be asking, where does this price come from? Most simply, prices are determined by how much of the good is available and how much of the good consumers demand.

Economics in an Afternoon

More will be said on this in the chapter about supply and demand.

How we value money is similar to how we value everything in our lives: if there is more of it we give it less value, if there is less of it then we value it more. This is why historically precious metals have made good currencies, the value of the metal being related to its relative rarity. This is also why, historically, soil never caught on as a currency; we value it so little that we literally

walk on it.

Though in modern

times we have taken a strange

turn from history and come up

with fiat currency. This is

currency that is in not backed up

by a commodity such as gold or

silver. Prior to fiat currency, you

could go to your local bank or

financial institution and trade in

your paper money for whatever

commodity (usually gold) that

backed up your currency. Now the

value fiat currency holds is solely

based on the faith and credibility that the people who use it are willing to give to it. In short: a dollar is worth a dollar because you and everyone around you says it is.

With the rise of fiat currency there has also been a rise in man-made inflation. Previously inflation usually only existed when a vast new source of gold was discovered, or a monarch recalled all the money in his realm, melted it down, and diluted it with some other metal of lesser value and re-issued the money.

Now governments can create their

own (metaphorical) gold mine by

simply printing, or even typing,

money into existence. This rise (or

inflation) of the supply of money is

what leads to a general rise in

prices (though not value) of goods,

this is often referred to as

inflation.

<u>Breaking Down the Matrix</u>

Earlier I mentioned a complex matrix of goods that all have a relative price with each other and how money simplifies the matrix enough to be able to make trades easily. Though the use of money simplifies everything, it does not make this vast network of relative prices disappear; it is all still there, silently working in the

background. Let's take a quick

peek at a small town to see how

this matrix continues to exist and

function despite money's

presence.

In this imaginary

town, called Townsville, most

people are farmers. Most of them

grow wheat, and very few grow

corn, yet there is only one person

who can repair the tractors that

the farmers use. To repair one

tractor the mechanic charges

$100. Wheat costs $10 per bushel,

Economics in an Afternoon

and corn costs $20. We may say
corn is twice as valuable as wheat.
Why can we make that statement?
Well you might think, look at the
price! Corn cost exactly twice as
much as wheat. That's true, but
why does wheat cost $10 and corn
$20? Well if we removed money
and the mechanic took payment in
grains, and would repair 1 tractor
for 10 bushels of wheat, and
would repair 1 tractor for only 5
bushels of corn, well we would still
say that corn is twice as valuable
as wheat.

Scott R. Hasserd

Now you might ask,

why is corn worth twice as much

as wheat? Well if the mechanic

can go to almost any farmer in

Townsville and obtain wheat from

them, yet only a few have corn for

sale, then the corn farmers can

charge a premium for their

product due to the scarcity of corn

in Townsville. Why can the corn

farmers do that? Because along

with the mechanic, the town

doctor, teacher, and mayor are all

lined up to purchase corn, and the

corn farmer only has a certain

amount of corn for sale, thus he
must charge higher prices to keep
from running out of corn. If he
sold the corn for $15 instead of
$20, the town police officer, school
principal, and fireman would also
be lined up to buy corn. This
would cause the farmer to run out
of corn before all of his customers
are satisfied. Whereas at $20 just
enough people buy corn that he
sells out of corn, yet there is no
one else in line to buy it, thus he
has met his supply of corn with
the town's demand for it perfectly,

this balance of supply and

demand is called equilibrium.

But why would some

people buy corn at $15 a bushel

and not at $20 per bushel?

Because for them it is simply not

worth it, which means that by

selling the corn at $20 the farmer

is ensuring that the corn only goes

to the people that value it the

most and thus making an efficient

use of the scarce supply at hand.

The Deal with Scarcity

Scarcity in economics simply means that there are infinite uses for a finite amount of a resource. For example, there is an infinite number of things I want to do with my time, but only so much time available. Therefore, I must have some way to prioritize which activities to do with my limited time. Time, in this instance, is scarce.

Although scarcity is related to a resource being finite, it is not the same. A good example of this is crude oil. Oil has always been a relatively finite resource; however, until it became popular as a fuel source for lamps and later machines, it was a burden in most cases. If you had a farm in pre-industrial America and crude oil started oozing up on your property, it was a disaster as this thick substance with little use would kill off your crops and your livelihood along with it. Oil in this instance was not scarce, it was simply finite. Scarcity only exists when there are more potential uses for something than the supply of it could fulfill.

An important note with scarcity is that it forces people to make choices between possible uses of scarce resources, thus by foregoing one option and instead choosing another, you are making a meaningful choice. Not every option available can be chosen;

compromises must be made. The option not chosen is what economists call "opportunity cost", which is what is given up when a choice is made. So if an energy provider has to make a choice between drilling two wells, one that would provide many barrels of oil, but very little natural gas, or one that has a few barrels worth of oil, but abundant natural gas, and they chose to drill at the site with many barrels of oil, the natural gas that they chose not to drill for (and the money made from selling it) is the opportunity cost for drilling at the oil rich site.

After crude oil began to be refined into products that appealed to the masses, such as in the case of Standard Oil refining crude into kerosene for lamps, crude oil was suddenly a scarce and valuable commodity, as opposed the bane of a farmer's existence. Scarcity is derived from demand, if there is no demand for something, then it is not scarce. The question is now asked, if scarcity exists, and there is infinite demand for finite resources, how do we answer the allocation problem every civilization faces, which is threefold:

- What gets produced?
- Who produces it?
- Who gets what is produced?

The answer: well it depends. The free market can run the economy, or a central planner (usually government) can run the economy.

<u>The Market Economy</u>

For the purposes of most economic arguments the term *free market* means a system where the individual can choose what to produce and how to spend the proceeds from selling the fruits of their labor, with some limitations. The four basic limitations that are most commonly suggested by economist for this purpose are:

- No use of deceit: this covers lying, cheating, and misleading

- No use of force: this covers theft and robbery

- Enforcement of Contracts: this ensures contracts will be followed

Those who argue for a market economy often argue that these three rules cover most of what is needed to make a stable, productive economy. But why?

Economics in an Afternoon

The first caveat is that
these three rules are assuming
that individuals have property
rights, which most economist
define as the right to own and use
property in any way you want,
short of causing harm to others.
History has shown us that
property rights are necessary to
create the proper incentives to
motivate people into being
productive players in an economy.
The market
economist's reasoning is that this
baseline will give everyone an

equal opportunity at success. The underlying idea or assumption is that the individual, who knows their own life the most intimately, will be the best informed to make decisions for their life given their situation.

Market economists will contend that markets serve to reconcile the demands of the consumer with the output of the supplier in a way that both the buyer and seller agree on. An example being that if you buy an apple from a vendor for a dollar, the two things were just

demonstrated: the first being that

you wanted the apple more than

the dollar, and the second being

the vendor wanted the dollar more

than the apple. Market economists

argue that this allows goods to be

allocated effectively based on

prices; prices serve to tell seller

where a good is most valued. If I

walked up during the previous

scenario and offered to buy the

apple for two dollars, then it tells

you and the vendor that I value

the apple at two dollars, and you

value it at one, this shows,

objectively, that I value the apple

more than you.

Market economist

believe that the answer to the

three questions of allocation are

best answered by the market, or in

other words, the population at

large, that chooses what to buy

and from whom, and this tells

producers what to make and sell.

The Planned Economy

Economists that advocate for planned economies, henceforth known as planners, argue that people are better off having the economy controlled by a central planner, usually the government, because the government has access to vast amounts of resources, information, and knowledge. The planning agency can expend the

time and effort to figure out how

best to use the nation's resources,

the planners would argue.

Sometimes planners often argue

on the basis that with the

government controlling prices and

wages, exploitation of the buyer

and the worker would be

prevented by the government.

Planners will also

state that by having the economy

be planned, the end result of the

economy is a more fair and equal

allocation of goods as one's need

will determine what they get and one's ability to produce will allow them to produce enough for themselves and others.

Planners would argue that if the goal of a successful economy is to truly make everyone better off, then the planning of the economy would allow for the less fortunate to not have to fear being exploited by the more fortunate and wealthier members of society, as prices and wages would be fixed in a way that would allow everyone to prosper, as everyone would have a level playing field in terms of benefits, wages, and prices.

The planning of the economy would also serve to liberate people as they would no longer have to worry about money and could focus on life without worrying about having to constantly acquire money and resources. With the planning of the economy, planners would be able to ensure that everyone gets to enjoy the fruits of everyone's labors without the wastefulness inherent in free markets.

A planned economy would allow for each individual to be entitled to as much as any other individual and not suffer from his or her own limitations and would thus allow for a more equitable society.

Whether via a market economy or a planned economy, the question of the allocation of resources is one that every society must answer. More and more countries are moving toward free market economies, usually called capitalist economies. Because of this, this type of economic system will be focused on for the rest of the book.

Supply and Demand

The concept of supply, demand, and their relationship to each other is essential to the understanding of any modern economy. Supply is simply the total amount of a good for sale, and demand is the total amount of the good that people want. Supply and demand allow us to compare and evaluate a good's relative scarcity and act accordingly. Most of the time, you even make that evaluation without even realizing it as you go about an average day.

For example, using price as a measure of relative scarcity, if you were to go to the store to purchase apples, yet to your surprise they are three times more expensive than you remember, and oranges are the same price as you remember, and much cheaper than apples, then you might opt to buy the oranges over the apples. The price of apples is higher than oranges because they are scarcer. Whether

a blight wiped out this year's apple

crop (a fall in supply), or suddenly

it is discovered they are a wonder

food and everyone wants more of

them (a rise in demand), apples

are scarcer, or to put it a bit

differently, more valuable. Due to

the price, you choose to act

accordingly to how scarce they are

without even realizing it!

An interesting note here is

how prices convey information,

and thus serve a role in

Scott R. Hasserd

coordinating resource allocation.
We will come back to that later.

It might be useful to
think of supply and demand as a
sort of conversation between a
buyer and a seller. The seller
wants a certain price for the goods
and the buyer wants another. How
they arrive at that price is not
arbitrary. The buyer may have a
myriad of other things he needs to
spend his money on, while the
seller has his expenses to cover
and a living that must be earned.
Thus, the seller wants to sell their

goods for the highest price possible and the buyer wants to buy the goods for the lowest price possible. These two people go back and forth in a discussion of the proper price, or at least one they can both agree on, before arriving to a conclusion. This is the function of the dialog between suppliers and demanders, to sort out a price for a good. Large scale supply and demand issues are simply this dialog, but aggregated to include everyone in the economy.

The Function and Role of Prices in Society

In the United States of America during the 70's there were two oil crises. In both cases, price controls seemed to be the root cause of the gasoline shortage in cities and glut in the country side. In the early 70's an OPEC oil embargo on the USA cause gas prices to triple or quadruple, and instead of allowing the price of oil

to naturally adjust, the
government in the US decided
implement price controls, which
caused a shortage, and then asked
everyone to simply drive less to
conserve oil before eventually
imposing a rationing system. If the
Government had simply let prices
rise, people would naturally use
less gas, because, as with
anything, the higher the price
goes, less and less people buy it.

So, if that is what
happens when prices are not
allowed to function, what happens

when they are allowed to perform

their role in society? The answer:

something just short of a miracle.

Let me elaborate. Let

us say there is a price for

platinum, which is a precious

metal that is used for a variety of

things in the industrial and

consumer world. Now let us say

you are a business owner who

uses platinum as a conductor in

some of your products. Imagine a

new mine in Uzbekistan is found

to have large platinum deposits,

and as a result the market is

flushed with platinum, the price drops and suddenly your products using platinum can now be extremely profitable now that the cost of platinum is lower and thus you invest more of your capital into growing that sector of your business. What just happened here? Without knowing about the new mine in Uzbekistan, just by watching the price, you acted as if you knew there was an increase in supply without knowing anything about the new mine; you just

Economics in an Afternoon

knew the price dropped and left you with larger profit margins.

Now for the reverse, imagine that the mine was not found, and instead a new use for platinum, or several platinum producing mines shut down all at once, or both, it does not matter. What does matter is that suddenly platinum has become scarcer and thus the price rose correspondingly. Now as a business owner, with platinum prices skyrocketing, you might look at ways to use less platinum (and thus conserving a scarce resource) or maybe using a less scarce resource such as gold or copper as a conductor in your product. In this scenario you have acted as though you knew that platinum was scarcer, without ever knowing the reason why.

The role prices play in society, when they are allowed to serve their purpose, is to convey information so that people may make meaningful economic decisions about how to use and conserve resources in ways that allocate goods to where they are used the most efficiently, and making the most of as little of a resource as possible. When price controls are implemented, prices cease to be able to serve their purpose as a conduit for information.

Scott R. Hasserd

Why Free Trade is a Big Deal

Current economic theory states that there are true gains to be had from free trade. This is based on the idea that one country produces what it produces best and the other produces what produces the least worst, and both will gain. Trade between countries can get complex, so I'll use an example

Economics in an Afternoon

using two people to illustrate how trading can be beneficial to both parties.

Let's say two people are stranded on a tropical island; Bob and Sue. In one hour, Bob can gather 10 coconuts or 4 fish. In that same hour Sue can gather 6 coconuts or 8 fish. So, assuming that they both don't want to eat only coconuts or only fish, then in an hour Bob can acquire 5 coconuts and 2 fish, Sue, on the other hand can gather 3 coconuts and 4 fish. However, if Bob decided to produce only coconuts and Sue only fish, and they traded, then Bob could trade 5 coconuts for 4 fish, thus Bob would end with 5 coconuts and 4 fish in one day, and Sue would end with 5 coconuts and 4 fish as well. Although it is a coincidence they both ended up with equal amounts of coconuts and fish, they both gained from the trade what they would otherwise not be able to produce. Bob had a net gain of 2 fish and Sue had a net gain of 2 coconuts. The total

number of food items produced
also went up because of the trade.
If Bob and Sue both divided their
time, then the total number of
coconuts plus fish between them
is 14 (8 coconuts plus 6 fish)
whereas when they stick to
producing what they make best
the total number of food items
jumps to 18 (10 coconuts plus 8
fish). These gains work whether
one party produces all goods
better than the other party or may
only produce one thing better than
the other party. This example was

only with two people, yet it holds true with whole nations as well.

One interesting topic in recent years has been the subject of trade deficits. This is simply when a country buys more in goods from other countries than it sells to them. Although this has been a point of contention, it is no different than when you go to a hardware store; you give them money, they give you goods. In terms of countries, goods flown in and capital (money) flows out, and vice versa. Just as you would go to

Economics in an Afternoon

a hardware store to buy lumber to

build a shed, a country might go

to another country to buy steel to

build a factory. Countries import

and buy things that it would be

more expensive to make, and thus

less efficient to produce, at home.

Thus, they can focus their

resources and labor on more

productive pursuits.

Scott R. Hasserd

What Inflation Is and Isn't

Sometimes in the news the CPI might get mentioned, what is that? The CPI stands for the Consumer Price Index, that is a "basket" of the most common consumer goods in an economy. So, for America things like a gallon of gas, gallon of milk, a dozen eggs, a loaf of bread, etc. would be included. Now the index part comes from averaging up these prices and tracking them over time. Thus, a rise or fall in the CPI is usually called inflation or deflation as it is usually seen as a general rise or fall in the average cost of goods. There are two problems with this in my estimation: the first with the CPI as a concept, and the second is my objection to what inflation really is.

The problem with the CPI as it is at the time of this writing, is best described by using the following metaphor: the average human body temperature is 98.6°F, if half of your body has a temperature of 0°F and the other half has a temperature of 197.2°F, then, on average, you are perfectly okay, right? Not by a long shot! The same is true with the CPI, if the price of gas falls through the floor, and the price of a gallon of water skyrockets, is the economy okay? Not likely!

The second problem with the CPI is that a general rise in prices is not inflation; it is the result of inflation. Milton

Economics in an Afternoon

Friedman is quoted as saying,

"Inflation is always and

everywhere a monetary

phenomenon in the sense that it is

and can be produced only by a

more rapid increase in the

quantity of money than in output,"

which I must admit, is a true

statement. It means that inflation

comes from increasing the amount

of money in the economy faster

than the economy is growing. Now

why might we need to increase the

money supply in the first place?

Central banks increase the money supply because they fear deflation.

While both deflation and inflation can be disastrous for an economy, and rampant inflation is seemingly more common, deflation has a worse reputation in most all economic courses and books. The reason for that being there are two types of deflation: natural and artificial. The artificial sort can really throw an economy into a death spiral as money rapidly becomes worth more and more causing the price of goods to

plummet, thus people and
companies refuse to spend money
as holding on to it seems to be a
better investment than spending
it, as it simply goes up and up in
value. However, the natural sort of
deflation happens when, as over
time, economies become more
efficient and productive and goods
simply become easier and more
streamlined to produce and
cheaper to sell. When cell phones
first came out they were as big as
bricks and were sold for just short
of $4,000! The first iPhone sold for

about $500! That sort of deflation is considered natural and healthy for an economy, though is sometimes might get conflated with the first, artificial sort.

The most stable solution between inflation and deflation seems to be a steadily rising money supply that grows slowly with the growth of the economy's output and thus price levels remain equal or almost equal throughout time.

<u>Why GDP is Important</u>

GDP stands for Gross Domestic Product and is the most common measure for an economy's growth and development. GDP is typically defined as the total amount of all *final* goods and services *produced* in an economy (things like used cars being sold, and lumber sold to make tables do not count). GDP is usually measured in US Dollars

Scott R. Hasserd

for consistency, though Nominal

GDP does not account for

variations in cost of living

(purchasing power) and other

expenses, such as inflation in an

economy, Real GDP accounts for

inflation and Purchasing Power

Parity (PPP) accounts for

differences in cost of living. GDP is

important because it is often used

to measure the productivity and

growth of a country's economy

and is used to compare different

countries' economies with one

another.